Conquering THE CHAOS
The Super Wonder Woman's 12-Step Strategy for a Stress FREELIFE

Conquering THE CHAOS

The Super Wonder Woman's
12-Step Strategy for a Stress FREELIFE

Michelle Clay, DO, CHHC

Founder and Visionary of FREELIFE7:
A Life Enhancing Company

CONQUERING THE CHAOS
Published by Purposely Created Publishing Group™
Copyright © 2018 Michelle Clay
All rights reserved.

No part of this book may be reproduced, distributed or transmitted in any form by any means, graphic, electronic, or mechanical, including photocopy, recording, taping, or by any information storage or retrieval system, without permission in writing from the publisher, except in the case of reprints in the context of reviews, quotes, or references.

Limit of Liability / Disclaimer of Warranty: While the publisher and author have used their best efforts in preparing this book, they make no representations or warranties with the respect to the accuracy or completeness of the contents of this book and specifically disclaim any implied warranties of fitness for a particular purpose. No warranty may be created or extended by sales representatives or written sales materials. The advice and strategies contained herein may not be suitable for your situation. You should consult with a doctor where appropriate. Neither the publisher nor author shall be liable for any loss or damages including but not limited to special, incidental, consequential or other damages.

Printed in the United States of America
ISBN: 978-1-948400-87-9

FREELIFE7 books and products are available through online book retailers. To contact Freelife7le.com directly, call our Customer Service Department within the US at 504-345-8671.

Table of Contents

Acknowledgments vii

Introduction: Let's Talk About Stress Baby! 1

Step 1: FREE Your Mind and the Rest
Will Follow 7

Step 2: Release the Past (Digestive Tract) 17

Step 3: Release Anger and Rage (Liver) 27

Step 4: Release Grief, Sadness, and Fear of
Life (Respiratory System/Lungs) 33

Step 5: Release Fear and Insecurity (Kidneys) 41

Step 6: Release Your Burdens (Musculoskeletal) 47

Step 7: Release Resistance (Reproductive) 53

Step 8: Release Bitterness and Annoyance
(Immune) 61

Step 9: Release Control (Endocrine) 69

Step 10: Release Anxiety (Skin) 77

Step 11: Release Unforgiveness and Bitterness (Heart) 83

Step 12: The Super Wonder Woman's Stress FREELIFE Strategy 89

Thank You 93

About the Author 97

Acknowledgments

I wrote this book for my sisters, Super Wonder Women. You know, the ones who ALWAYS answer the call when no one else can; you are dependable, and you get the job done. You're the executive, wife, mother, partner, entrepreneur, physician, daughter, sister, bestie, soror, bonus mom and she-ro who can regulate and rescue everyone and everything except YOU! You're the CEO of companies but have been unable to be the CEO of your life, your peace, or your calm. Though we can leap tall expectations in a single bound, we've been unable to conquer the burnout, stress, and overwhelm that results from fulfilling the tall orders and expectations of 'success,' and we suffer silently. Every day, we get up, beat our face, snatch our wig, put on our three-inch heels, and slay, and no one knows. I get it. I get you. I *am* you.

My journey to this point has been full of failures and successes, setbacks and comebacks, joy and tears, pain, passion, and purpose. I've been stressed out before and even contemplated suicide, but it wasn't until I embarked on the journey of becoming a bonus mom on the backdrop of holding down a job, business, doctor, relationship, and three households that it all came tumbling down and my she-ro shoulders buckled. I was called upon to do more than just love and care for a child that I didn't birth. I had to create a Super Wonder Woman shield to deflect the fiery arrows from the ex and balance being in the middle of a tug-of-war for the affection and attention of the child between the parents. My uterine fibroid grew to the size of a grapefruit, my neck locked up, and I developed gallstones. Eating all raw foods at the time was not enough; my health still deteriorated. I had to create some different Super Wonder Woman powers to conquer this chaos and reclaim my calm. In all things, I give gratitude, because what my health issues did was ignite a journey of self-healing, connections, harmony, and a revolutionary mindset that brought me a peace that surpassed my understanding. It silenced the broken record of negative self-chatter, released me from the silent, stress-filled suffering, and removed the roadblocks to an unapologetically passionate and happy stress FREELIFE! And I want to share these superpowers with you! When you are overwhelmed and just plain 'over it' and you start feeling these unexplained aches, pains, and breakdowns, you'll know why, but most importantly, you'll know what to do. Add these superpowers to your Super Wonder Woman tool belt that you may rescue your health, harmony, and happiness so you can truly live YOUR FREELIFE on purpose and with passion.

Yours in Health and Harmony,
Dr. Michelle

Introduction: Let's Talk About Stress, Baby!

Let's talk about stress, baby! People often think of stress as an emotional response, something you need to get over, or a sign of weakness. Through my research, study, and personal journey, I discovered that there is a scientific cause of stress with a physiological response. People might tell you, "I'm too blessed to be stressed," but science doesn't support that—especially when the stress response is designed for our benefit. It is designed to protect us and give us the surge of energy necessary for our survival in dangerous situations and during a time crunch.

Stress is a normal part of life that is designed for our survival, either to enhance our performance or protect us from threats. In today's non-stop world, our perception of threats to our sense of well-being and pain, both physical and emotional, are encountered daily. Whether it is job security or satisfaction, unhealthy relationships, challenging family dynamics, or illness of ourselves or a loved one, our brain perceives a threat and responds with the stress response for prolonged periods of time, making you feel your brain is overloaded and never shuts off. What was designed to facilitate our escape from harm and danger temporarily is being activated repeatedly on a chronic basis.

Stress activates that "Oh caca" response known as the "fight or flight" response when we perceive danger or threat by either fighting or running. In the short-term, we can adapt to the stress to maintain balance or homeostasis by eliminating or avoiding the stressor or challenge. Over time, in a chronic stressful situation, maintaining physiological stability and balance becomes more difficult. Chronic stress, extraordinary levels of stress, or repeated exposure to stressors can lead to wear and tear and affect every system in your body. It can make you more vulnerable to serious mental and physical diseases, such as high blood pressure, diabetes, high cholesterol, impaired immunity, and infertility. You know the saying "Mind over matter"?

Prolonged stress affects your mindset, making it difficult to think clearly, have the confidence to live in your purpose, or the calm to even just make it day to day.

So, what exactly are stress and the stress response?

There is part of our nervous system called the **autonomic nervous system (ANS)**, which is responsible for processes that automatically occur without us thinking about them, such as digestion, heart rate, blood pressure, and body temperature regulation.

Two branches of the ANS that regulate the stress or "fight or flight" response and balance are:

1. Sympathetic Nervous System – "fight or flight" to prepare us to handle potential danger or pain.
2. Parasympathetic Nervous System – "rest and digest" to return us to a state of homeostasis or balance once the threat of danger or pain has passed.

The ANS is controlled by the hypothalamus, or the "Master Gland," located in the brain. The hypothalamus receives the message, "Danger, danger! Oh caca!!"

and transmits that signal to every system in the body via our fiber-optic network—the nervous system.

Now for a little anatomy and physiology lesson. I feel it is important to empower people with information to activate their transformation! When people have a better understanding of their bodies, the light bulb comes on (an "AHA" moment), and they can make better, healthier, and happier decisions.

Once the hypothalamus registers, "Danger! Danger! Run! Get out! Oh caca!" it activates the sympathetic nervous system for "fight or flight"—your stress response. The stress response initiates a cascade of events that results in an increased production of the hormone cortisol, which is our "stress hormone." High cortisol levels result in numerous changes in our body, including our way of thinking, outlook on life, weight, and blood pressure.

This 12-step strategy guides you through a journey of self-discovery and self-awareness. It empowers you to be more aware of the challenges that trigger your stress and connect how they make you feel and how they affect your health and well-being. It assists in revealing the emotions and mindsets you have been holding on to that have been holding you back from your "release-and-relax" Zen moment. This 12-step guide provides tools to strategically release them system by system and step by step with a culinary cure to recharge your wellness and affirmations to shift to a stress-FREE mindset. Mindset is BAE. Mindset is EVERYTHING. In the words of another Super Wonder Woman, Maya Angelou, "When you know better, you do better!"

STEP 1:
FREE Your Mind and the Rest Will Follow

I remember a commercial for the United Negro College Fund (UNCF) that said, "A mind is a terrible thing to waste." It is also a terrible thing to be locked into the same way of perceiving things. If you can elevate your brain health and free your mind of worry and angst, your FREELIFE will follow! Before you can free your mind, you must have an understanding of the function of the brain.

Function of Brain/Nervous System
The nervous system allows us to perceive and respond to both our internal and external environment, as well as control all our bodily functions, such as breathing, heartbeat, digestion, and movement. It is composed of

two parts: the central nervous system (CNS) and the peripheral nervous system (PNS). The central nervous system is made up of the brain and spinal cord. The peripheral nervous system is made up of nerves that branch off the spinal cord to connect and communicate with organs and muscles of all parts of the body; it is the body's electrical system, or fiber optics more connected than AT&T. Think of the brain as your control center; your favorite computer that has ALL your important documents on it. The brain weighs approximately three pounds and is the seat of intelligence, consciousness, communication, body movement, and behavior.

The PNS is further divided into the somatic and autonomic nervous system.

The somatic portion of the nervous system is responsible for voluntary movement—like walking, jumping, push-ups, sit-ups, and reflexes. It also receives sensory information such as pain so that you can move your body to safety.

The autonomic nervous system is involuntary. Its primary function is to maintain homeostasis or balance of our bodies. It accomplishes this by regulating things such as temperature, heart rate, blood pressure,

digestion, and fluid balance. It is composed of the parasympathetic nervous system, which controls body functions for "rest and digest," and the sympathetic nervous system, which controls the "fight or flight" or the stress response. When we encounter danger or any kind of threat, it is the sympathetic nervous system that is activated. Changes occur in our bodies as a result of the increased level of cortisol, such as increased heart rate, increased blood pressure, increased blood flow to our muscles, decreased digestion, and increased production of glucose or blood sugar to provide the energy to move and respond quickly. These are all necessary responses to help us survive. With a temporary threat and/or stress trigger, our bodies can easily adapt and return to homeostasis (balance) once the threat is removed or ends. However, with chronic stress, or when you are being triggered repeatedly for long periods of time, your body does not have an opportunity to return to homeostasis. Blood pressure and blood sugar levels may remain elevated, making you more vulnerable to developing chronic disease. Not only does chronic stress affect your physical body, but also your brain health and your mental and emotional outlook.

Effect of Stress on Nervous System

Impaired Memory

The hippocampus is the area of the brain most susceptible to stress. It is responsible for short- to intermediate-term memory of people, places, and things; learning; and emotional regulation. Prolonged stress destroys nerve cells in this area, causing it to decrease in size. Wondering why you keep forgetting where you placed your keys? Maybe it is the constant stress you are under from increased work responsibilities. This is reversible following a return to relaxation and homeostasis.

Increased Fear and Anxiety

The amygdala is the area of the brain known as the fear center. It is responsible for perception of a threat. Stress increases the activity of this area of the brain, causing anxiety, panic, fear, and/or anger. There is a stress-anxiety disorder link.

Impaired Judgement, Reasoning, Long-Term Planning, and Self-Discipline

The frontal cortex of the brain is responsible for the above thought processes. It is located where your forehead is. It is the largest part of the brain and does not fully mature until 25 years old. It is most influenced by experiences. Stress shrinks nerve cells in this area. That is why, for instance, when you are in the middle of a chronic life challenge, it is often difficult to see the light at the end of the tunnel or make a plan to shift the situation. Also, don't be so frustrated with your children when they don't know what they "want to be when they grow up"; their brains are not even fully developed. No, they don't have a plan and are having difficulty making one; cut them a little slack.

Decreased Pleasure

The dopamine system in the brain is associated with pleasure and reward to things such as food, sex, and social interactions and tells a person what it did to receive that pleasure so that they can repeat it. The more motivated and interested we are or pleasure we receive from an activity, the more dopamine is released and the more we remember it. The reward center helps us to stay focused and repeat activities that were reinforced through positive outcomes. Stress depletes dopamine pathways, resulting in decreased sense of pleasure, lack of motivation or drive, low mental energy, and lack of enthusiasm.

There is a stress-depression link.

Culinary Cure for the Stressed-Out Brain

High-Antioxidant Foods

Foods that are rich in antioxidants, such as blueberries, may help protect nerve cells that use dopamine from damage. Blueberries have been linked to improvements in learning, thinking, and memory.

Cinnamon

Cinnamon has been shown to improve memory, increase attention, and enhance cognitive processing. You don't have to consume cinnamon to enjoy these benefits. Just the aroma of cinnamon can give you a lift and a sense of calm. In addition, cinnamon has been shown to have antioxidant, anti-diabetic, and anti-bacterial properties. Cinnamon slows the rate at which the stomach empties, thus reducing the rise in blood sugar after eating and improving insulin sensitivity, which is often compromised in people with type 2 diabetes. This, in turn, helps with the regulation of blood sugar, which can be compromised with chronic stress. It's a win-win all the way around; pleasant odor, healthier brain, and sweet taste without making diabetes worse.

Mindset

Albert Einstein said, "You can't solve a problem with the same mind that created it." To release stress requires a shift in your mindset. Mindset is everything! First, you must recognize that you have these feelings and symptoms. Then you must have the desire and commitment to shift to your next and best self.

A great place to start is with visualization. Visualization is imagining and seeing exactly what it is you want in your mind. Basically, if you can see it, you can be it and have it. Brain studies reveal that thoughts produce the same mental instructions as actions.

Visualization reduces stress, increases confidence, and primes your brain for success. To enjoy the full benefits of visualization, not only should you see, but you should feel, taste the pleasant flavors, and smell the sweetness. Activate all your senses!

Picture your perfect day and/or the life of your dreams. Or simply visualize your peaceful, calm, and stress-free self. What does it look like? What do you smell? Can you feel a warm breeze on your face? Is the wind blowing through your hair? Is your favorite song playing? Where are you? How do you feel? Engage all your senses as if you are living that moment; you have already achieved your goal and are living the life of your wildest and joyous imagination! By going through it in your mind, you put it into motion. If your mind can conceive it, you have already achieved it!

Now couple those thoughts and images with the words that you speak. That is why affirmations are so powerful, especially when you begin with "I am." Speaking "I am" initiates the creative process.

Affirmations

"My mind is becoming calm and clear."

"I am releasing my worries."

"I control my thoughts and feelings. I tell my mind what to think."

"My thoughts are calm and under control."

"My mind is tranquil, serene, and stress free."

"I think positively and clearly, even in stressful situations."

"This is only for a moment. This too shall pass quickly."

"I can see stressful situations as positive challenges."

Using these affirmations with visualization will help you free your mind of stress, worry, and anxiety and let your calm, serene, and peaceful FREELIFE follow.

STEP 2:
Release the Past (Digestive Tract)

"Forgiveness is giving up the hope that the past could have been any different."

–Oprah Winfrey

Many people live more in their past than they do in their present. You play an argument from the past on repeat in your head, wishing you could say something different. Or, "If only I had _____ (fill in the blank), my life would be much different." According to Louise Hay, there is a correlation between holding on to things in the past and digestive health.

Function of the Digestive System

Digestion begins with chewing with the teeth. Once you have chewed then swallowed, the food, which is now called a food bolus, moves to the esophagus. From the esophagus, it moves to the stomach, where digestive juices and enzymes further break down the food bolus. There is an extremely powerful acid, hydrochloric acid (HCl), inside of your stomach that is part of this process. Outside of the body, HCl is so powerful, it can eat a hole through a cement floor! The next stop on the digestion pathway is the intestinal tract.

The intestinal tract is made up of two main parts—the small intestine and the large intestine or colon. Connected to the stomach, the small intestine is where most of the digestive process takes place. Not only does it break down food, it is also responsible for absorbing vital and necessary vitamins and nutrients from the food you eat and returns them to the bloodstream to help fuel other necessary body functions. It is 22 feet in length—the longest portion of the digestive system.

The large intestine, also called the colon, is where water is absorbed and any remaining food that has been extracted of its nutrients, bacteria, and other waste is formed into feces. This is then released from our bodies through bowel movements. The colon is shorter than the small intestine, measuring six feet in length. Waste is moved through the small intestine, then the colon, then the rectum to exit the body through an involuntary muscle movement called peristalsis.

What happens to the digestive system with stress?

During episodes of increased stress or chronic stress, the intestinal tract can respond in a variety of ways. Stress can cause decreased absorption of nutrients in the small intestine, decreased blood flow to the digestive tract, which decreases the metabolism (my comrades over 40 can relate to that), and even changes in peristalsis, leading to diarrhea or constipation.

Esophagus

When you're stressed, you "stress eat." We've all done it at one point or another. You go for sweets like a pint of butter pecan ice cream or my favorite, those salty and crunchy snacks like chips. The crunch will make it all better and go away right? WRONG! Chronic stress increases your probability of experiencing reflux, and you increase the probability even more by choosing comfort foods that actually make you feel more uncomfortable. If you already have a diagnosis of gastroesophageal reflux disease (GERD), psychological stressors can increase heartburn symptoms. Studies indicate that the amount of reflux doesn't increase during stress, but the likelihood of feeling a reflux as heartburn does increase.

Stomach

When you're stressed, your brain becomes more alert to sensations in your stomach. We've all experienced it. Before the biggest presentation of your life, you may feel "butterflies" in your stomach or even nausea or pain. If your stress and anxiety level is high enough, you may even vomit. If you have a big presentation or job interview, this is a temporary stress response, which is completely normal. Notice that after the event or situation has concluded, those symptoms go away. However, with chronic stress, there is an increased production of acid in the stomach, which possibly could lead to the development of ulcers (gastric ulcers) or severe stomach pain without ulcers.

Intestines

Chronic stress affects digestion. There are muscles that line the inside of our intestinal tract that are not under our control (involuntary). They move to actively push digested food and waste along the intestinal tract until you eventually release the waste through a bowel movement. This process is called peristalsis. With chronic stress, peristalsis will either slow down, leading to constipation, or speed up, resulting in diarrhea. People diagnosed with Irritable Bowel Syndrome (IBS) experience alternating diarrhea, constipation, and abdominal pain.

The health and relaxation of the intestinal tract are important for your mental state and sense of well-being. This is what is known as the gut-brain axis. Research shows that the brain influences the intestinal tract as much as the intestinal tract influences brain activity. (There is a bidirectional communication link.) We have bacteria that naturally live in our digestive tract (gut) that are beneficial. These bacteria, also known as the microbiome, are responsible for regulating digestion and metabolism (breakdown and processing of food and nutrients) and extracting vitamins from the food we eat.

The population and balance of beneficial versus harmful bacteria are influenced by many factors. Factors like environment, stress, anxiety, depression, processed foods, and a diet that is dominated by sugar and carbohydrates will alter the bacterial balance of the intestinal tract and can wreak havoc. Nervous emotional stress alters the balance of beneficial and harmful bacteria. Gut bacteria also produce hundreds of neurochemicals that the brain uses to regulate mental processes such as learning, memory, and mood. Ninety-five percent of one very important neurochemical or neurotransmitter, serotonin, which influences mood and the activity in the digestive system, is produced in the digestive tract. There are more serotonin receptors in the gut than there are in our brains. It is as if the gut has its own brain. Ever notice how when you are stressed out or nervous, your bowel habits change?

Culinary Cure for the Stressed-Out Gut

The three main ingredients for the health of your digestive tract, stress-less demeanor, and calmer mood are fiber, prebiotics, and probiotics.

Fiber

Fiber acts like a broom to sweep out the inside of your intestinal tract. It is optimal to consume 25 mg – 35 mg of fiber per day for digestive health. Green, leafy vegetables and fruit with the edible skin are always the better option for fiber intake as opposed to supplements, especially when consumed raw.

Prebiotics

There are certain foods that pass directly into the large intestine or colon without being partially digested in the small intestine. These are called prebiotics. These substances are important because they provide a food source for beneficial bacteria to use, grow, and multiply. Prebiotics also help lower cortisol levels and the stress response. Examples of food sources of prebiotics are onions and raw garlic.

Probiotics

Probiotics have gotten more attention lately, especially with the popularity of kombucha products. To help maintain a healthy balance, consuming fermented foods and food or supplements with live bacteria, such as kombucha and Greek yogurt, can help.

Releasing your stress helps both your emotional and digestive health. Because the mind and body are connected, a shift in mindset and release of stress could be just what the doctor ordered for improved digestive health.

Mindset

Per Louise Hay, bowel problems are related to fear of letting go. Constipation specifically is associated with refusing to release old ideas. I had a friend who was diagnosed with Irritable Bowel Syndrome (IBS), a condition affecting the colon, which includes symptoms of diarrhea, constipation, cramping, bloating, and/or abdominal pain. It is listed in the Diagnostic and Statistical Manual of Mental Illness (DSM-V), the classification for mental disorders. Going out and sharing a meal with my friend used to be a challenge. My friend started counseling and developed strategies to come to terms with issues stemming from the divorce of her parents at a young age, a strained relationship with her father, and a challenging dynamic with her mother. After months of counseling to reach some resolution, the symptoms of IBS ceased.

What from your past is holding you back from your bright and brilliant future?

What scenario or conversation is playing over and over in your head that you just can't shake?

Are you ready to release and let it go?

Affirmations

"I freely and easily release the old and joyously welcome the new."

"I choose to let go of the past and embrace the present moment."

"I know that old, negative patterns no longer limit me. I release them with ease."

"Do not let the future be held hostage by the past."
–Neal A Maxwell

STEP 3
Release Anger and Rage (Liver)

Many have pent-up anger that they do not release on a regular basis. Every time you don't express your true feelings and release, the anger builds up until it turns into full-blown rage and explodes like a volcano. While this is happening, your physical body is experiencing the same thing on the cellular level. There is a connection between unreleased anger and resentment and the optimal functioning of the liver.

Function of the Liver

The function of the liver is to cleanse the blood and remove toxic substances that we've eaten, inhaled, or rubbed on our bodies. Our entire blood supply passes through the liver several times per day. It performs over 500 functions, such as filtering bacteria from blood and producing enzymes necessary for digestion. When you are under a significant amount of physical or mental stress, your liver can become overworked and overloaded.

What happens to the liver with stress?

Chronic stress causes the liver to produce more blood sugar or glucose. This can be dangerous for those who are pre-diabetic or suffering from diabetes. On a personal note, the pain I felt in the area of my liver is what led me to this work of creating simple and natural stress-releasing strategies. It was summer, and we had two two-week visits with my bonus child with three weeks in between. What made the visits so challenging was the long 15-hour drive one way to pick up the child and deal with massive drama once we arrived. The simple solution would be to meet at a specific place at a specific time to pick up the child, so we could rest, enjoy each other, and go on our way. But no, the time and place always changed. We would get to one location, wait, and then receive a message to go somewhere else. It was like a scavenger hunt for a child; all of this while just getting

Conquering the Chaos

off a 15-hour road trip! This was not the first time this had happened. Trying to be a loving and supportive mate, I often was a sounding board for my partner so he could vent. I was patient and offered words of encouragement. Inside, I was seething! All kinds of four-letter words and expletives were rolling around in my head. But I kept silent. The conversation of the ex and the frustration from the manipulative tactics being done with the child continued before we went to sleep, when we woke up, and sometimes throughout the day. I had had enough, but I wanted to be a "good" and supportive partner. Just because you don't express the feelings, doesn't mean they aren't there. Daily, I started having pain in my liver area. Then the heartburn began. How could this be? I was only eating watermelon, salad, and kale! I discovered I had gallstones. The gall bladder is a small, sac-like organ that sits under the liver. Gallstones commonly develop in people with the "4 Fs": Female, Fat, Forty, and Fertile.

Culinary Cures

Cruciferous Vegetables

Cruciferous vegetables are rich in sulfur compounds, which help the body produce glutathione. Glutathione is a compound that is necessary for the liver to cleanse harmful toxins. Chronic stress can decrease your levels of glutathione. When something or someone is on your "last nerve," have some broccoli. Broccoli is a cruciferous vegetable that is a great source of Vitamin C, which helps level out those cortisol spikes.

Lemons

Drinking freshly-squeezed lemon or lime juice in the morning helps stimulate the liver and boost production of the liver detoxification enzymes that help flush out carcinogens and other toxins. The beauty is that while you are cleansing your liver, you are also managing your stress. Lemons are an excellent source of

Vitamin C. Studies have shown that consuming 1000 mg of Vitamin C per day can help mitigate the stress response by decreasing cortisol levels. So, before you rush off to work and encounter that horrid traffic and insane drivers, drink your warm lemon water. It will help turn road rage into road calm.

Mindset

Per Louise Hay, the liver is the organ associated with resistance to change, fear, and anger. Sometimes what stresses people out is resisting changes that occur in life instead of flowing with them or being the change agent.

There is a song by Quincy Jones sung by James Ingram called "Everything Must Change."

> Everything must change
> Nothing stays the same
> Everyone will change
> No one stays the same
> The young become the old
> And mysteries do unfold
> 'Cause that's the way of time
> Nothing and no one goes unchanged

There is nothing wrong with anger. Problems arise when pent-up anger has not been released in a constructive and positive manner. Sometimes change and the resistance to it produces anger. Surrender and embrace change instead of being angered by it.

Release the anger and resentment that can result in stress instead of holding on to it.

Affirmations

"I release old hurt, anger, and resentment easily."

"I have great peace within and nothing shall offend me."

"I deserve only happiness and now am free of anger. I live and let live. I am in control of my life."

"I am a strong Super Wonder Woman and shall remain calm and poised at all times."

STEP 4:
Release Grief, Sadness, and Fear of Life (Respiratory System/Lungs)

"I believe that every single event in life happens in an opportunity to choose love over fear."

–Oprah Winfrey

Have you ever had a traumatic or stressful event that felt like it took your breath away? Sucked the life out of you? Left you feeling fearful to live life fully, but instead play it safe and stay safe? Breath is life, and when you feel deep sadness and despair as if the life has been sucked out of you, you need to understand the respiratory system.

Function of Respiratory System

The respiratory system is responsible for a mandatory element of life—breathing. Breath is life! The respiratory system is composed of the nose, sinuses, pharynx, larynx, trachea, diaphragm, and of course, the lungs. Breathing is really about gas exchange, exchanging oxygen (O_2) for carbon dioxide (CO_2). We breathe in air through either our nose or our mouth. The nose and sinus passages are responsible for warming, filtering, and humidifying (adding moisture) to this air. It then passes through to the pharynx. What is so interesting is both food and air pass through the pharynx. What determines which path they travel from there is the gatekeeper—the glottis. The glottis is like a door made of cartilage. When the glottis opens, air is allowed to pass to its next destination—the larynx. The glottis closes when food is going through the pharynx and passes to the esophagus for digestion. This step is very important. If the glottis opens even slightly when eating, it allows food to pass to the larynx, resulting in choking. This is what is referred to as "passing down the wrong pipe." From the larynx, air moves through the trachea, which is commonly referred to as the "wind pipe." The trachea then splits into two branches called bronchi for air to enter the right and the left lung. Here is where the magic happens! Red blood cells pick up oxygen from the lungs and travel to the heart to be pumped throughout our bodies through arteries to deliver oxygen-rich blood to our cells and organs to maintain function. The red blood cells are the transport system. Once at the cells, red blood cells deliver the oxygen molecules and pick up carbon dioxide (CO_2), which is the cell's waste, to go in the reverse through veins and leave our bodies when we exhale. Wow! So, do not "wait to exhale," as stated in Terry McMillan's book. Breathe! Breath is life, and every inhale and exhale are your life and your peace of mind.

Effect of Stress on Lungs

Chronic stress causes inflammation and constriction or narrowing of these small passages through which air moves called bronchoconstriction. This causes worsening symptoms of asthma and chronic lung diseases, such as chronic obstructive pulmonary disease (COPD), emphysema, and chronic bronchitis.

Culinary Cures

Flavonoids

Flavonoids have anti-inflammatory properties. One named catechin helps decrease inflammation, and therefore constriction, of the airways worsened by chronic stress. A good source of this flavonoid is green tea. Green tea suppresses the spike in the stress response. It is used for stress relief and the treatment of anxiety and improves concentration and focus, which often are compromised when your brain is burdened by stress and worry.

Folate

Folate is in the family of B vitamins, specifically B9. Research shows people suffering from increased breathlessness from COPD, emphysema, and bronchitis have low folate levels. Increasing folate could benefit these individuals by offering some protection and improving lung function. Folate is also necessary for brain and nerve function. Remember the stress response begins in the brain, which is part of the nervous system. Therefore, folate is necessary for your stress release protocol. Dietary sources of folate include green, leafy vegetables and black beans.

Mindset

I don't have a chronic lung condition, but I have had the experience of a life-changing event that left me feeling deep sadness and fearful of the future. How was I going to live life now? What would the future be like? When I was in my internship after graduating from medical school, I received a call one night from my little brother. He requested my address to send me what he called the "last letter of his life." I talked with him and prayed with him, and we read scripture together. I went to sleep feeling peaceful that he was going to be alright. Hours later, I was awakened by the phone ringing. It was my mother. She could barely talk from crying. All I could make out was "Teddy." He was gone. My mother came home from her night job to music blasting in the house and my brother lying in the garage, a gun next to him and a puddle of blood under his head. I was in shock! I couldn't believe I had just spoken to him a few hours earlier. I thought my prayers had been answered. I thought we had prayed for his peace of mind and excitement for his future life. I flew home the next day. My cousin picked me up from the airport and took me home. When I walked into the house and saw my mother's eyes, they looked like shadows; life was missing from her eyes, just as her baby son's life was no more. That's when I realized it was real, and it felt like my breath was sucked from my chest. For the last 21 years of my life, I had been the "big sister." I was his protector, source of practical jokes, and sometimes his confidant, as only siblings can be. What was life going to be like in the future? He was only 21 years old, and he never got an opportunity to be husband or father. I never got an opportunity to be his children's favorite aunt. It felt like my breath was gone for an hour. Then my mother hugged me, my cousin put his arms around both of us, and I finally felt an exhale. I was still here.

Per Louise Hay, lung problems are associated with depression, sadness, grief, or fear of life. Exactly. Breathe your way through it. Most if not all breathing exercises stimulate our body and mind into a state of balance (homeostasis) and "rest & digest." Breathing exercises can oxygenate the blood, which aids in the elimination of toxins from the lungs and the entire system, which in turn improves physical and mental health. Deep diaphragmatic breathing (belly breathing) creates relaxation and peace of mind, keeping you in the present moment. This is mindfulness.

Most of the time when we are experiencing stress or anxiety, we automatically hold our breath. Stop! Become aware of your breath—your life. Inhale fully, then exhale fully.

Affirmations

"I am moving through grief to embrace other emotions."

"I can hold on to the love and let go of the grief."

"I have the capacity to take in the fullness of life."

"I lovingly live life to the fullest."

STEP 5:
Release Fear and Insecurity (Kidneys)

"Insecurity is self-sabotage. If you want to fly, you have to first see your wings."

—Unknown

The practice of traditional Chinese Medicine (TCM) is based on the premise that our Qi, or life force energy, should be balanced. The absence of a creative or constructive way to express repressed and unreleased emotions can result in the imbalance of Qi in the organs with which those emotions are associated. Feelings of fear, insecurity, and lack of confidence to move forward are associated with the kidneys.

Function of Kidneys

The kidneys are bean-shaped organs approximately the size of a fist. The adrenal glands sit on top of them. The kidneys are a powerful filtration system for blood. All the blood in our body passes through the kidneys several times a day via an artery called the renal artery. The kidneys are made up of hundreds of thousands small filtration units called nephrons. This is where the actual filtration takes place. The nephrons filter out the waste and send necessary nutrients back through the body via the bloodstream. Kidneys also control the body's fluid balance, contribute to blood pressure regulation, and regulate the balance of electrolytes such as potassium and sodium. Every day, the kidneys process about 150 quarts of blood to sift out about two quarts of waste from body processes, such as metabolism, and by-products of toxins that get into our bodies. The waste and extra water become urine. This waste and water flow out of the kidneys through a small tube called a ureter, allowing it to flow into the bladder and pass out of the body as urine.

Effect of Stress on Kidneys

Mental and emotional stress can decrease the amount of blood flow through the kidneys and the amount of sodium removed from the body. This affects the amount of toxicity removed from the body, which can negatively impact your entire system and overall health.

Prolonged periods of stress can exacerbate diabetes via production of more blood sugar and insulin resistance. It can also contribute to high blood pressure. Both chronic diseases affect kidney health. Not to mention that most people's drug of choice for stress are high-sugar or salty foods, further contributing to the problem. There is also a correlation between long-standing stress and kidney stones.

Culinary Cure

Water

Our bodies are approximately 70 percent water. You must give the kidneys something to work with to produce adequate amounts of urine to remove toxins from our bodies and keep things flowing. Adequate hydration is necessary to reduce and manage stress because even a mild dehydration of 1 percent of your body weight can affect your mood. If you feel thirsty, it's too late; you are already dehydrated. Drink some water and calm down.

Parsley

Parsley can be used as a natural diuretic to help relieve water retention and ease bloating.

Parsley benefits kidney health because it helps stimulate the production of urine (and kidney function). Parsley is a rich source of zinc, which helps reduce stress by inhibiting the release of cortisol.

Mindset

You wouldn't know it, but I am an incognito insecure person. Shhh! Don't tell anyone. I've hidden it by excelling in school and being the "dependable" one, the one who gets the praises and accolades for "doing the right thing." I have missed opportunities in my life because I was too insecure to trust in my power and abilities, and I listened to the sabotaging voice inside that said, "You can't do that. It will be too hard. You're not good enough." A lot of affirmations, both said to myself and from others, are what made the difference.

When the negative self-chatter starts with those "gremlins" saying you are not enough, replace it with "I am _____" to counteract those thoughts and create a new reality. With all that I have accomplished, I still do this every day.

Affirmations

"On the other side of my fear is freedom."

"I choose to love and approve of myself."

"I offer a lot to the world."

"Only good comes from each experience."

"The light of a new day always chases the shadows of the night away and shows us that the shape of our fear is only the ghost of our own minds." –Terry Goodkind

STEP 6:
Release Your Burdens (Musculoskeletal)

For the Super Wonder Women who do it all to have it all, you carry your load and often the load of others. After a while, the weight is too heavy to carry any longer because your shoulders begin to hurt, your back begins to ache, and/or your joints begin to creak and crunch. Most of the time, a Super Wonder Woman is a one-woman she-ro holding down the fort and has difficulty asking for help, even though she has grown weary of carrying the weight and responsibility of the world on her shoulders. To be stronger, it is necessary to release her burdens; to release and let go of what has been weighing her down.

Function of Musculoskeletal System

The musculoskeletal system consists of muscles, bones, joints, ligaments, tendons, and cartilage. There are 206 bones, 650 muscles, and 187 joints in the human body. The main functions of the musculoskeletal system are:

- Support
- Protection of the internal organs and structures
- Movement (muscles)
- Production of red and white blood cells from the bone marrow
- Storage of calcium (in the bones)

Effect of Stress on Muscles and Bones

One of the most common physical symptoms of stress that people notice first is muscle tension—usually a stiff neck or a tight knot in the muscle of your shoulder (supraspinatus). You know that feeling of sitting at your desk after a 10-hour day and it feels like a golf ball back there? Yes, that most likely is stress. Stress and emotional conflict can stimulate pain and tension in the muscles of the neck, face, scalp, and jaw.

Overwhelming stress can contribute to an increased frequency of headaches, including what is known as a muscle tension headache. Muscle tension headaches can also be caused by depression, anxiety, eye strain, or lack of sleep.

Not only are your muscles affected by stress, but your joints are as well. For those who suffer from arthritis, stress may intensify the pain. Some studies have shown a correlation between job dissatisfaction and depression and back problems.

Culinary Cure

Foods that have anti-inflammatory properties such as turmeric can help bring relief to tense muscles and inflamed joints in arthritis. For bone health, foods high in calcium and magnesium are beneficial.

Turmeric

Turmeric is considered the "Golden Goddess" in Ayurvedic medicine. What gives turmeric its bright yellow color is its active ingredient called curcumin. It has a wide array of health benefits, including anti-bacterial and anti-inflammatory properties. Numerous studies show that turmeric is helpful for relieving symptoms of rheumatoid arthritis by decreasing the inflammation. Turmeric's active component, curcumin, has also shown promise as an antidepressant. Studies have shown that curcumin enhances nerve growth in areas of the brain associated with emotional equilibrium and boosts the "feel good" neurotransmitters (biochemicals) serotonin and dopamine. Serotonin regulates your mood, and dopamine is responsible for pleasure and pain. During times of chronic stress, levels of dopamine, our "pleasure" chemical, decreases.

Magnesium

Magnesium is necessary for muscle contraction as well as the process of building up and breaking down of bone. During episodes of stress, magnesium is lost from the cells. The more stressful an event is perceived or the longer the stress response is activated, the more magnesium is depleted. Magnesium helps reduce stress by blocking the part of the nervous system that is responsible for the stress response, the sympathetic nervous system, which leads to relaxation. Magnesium also helps balance the body's production of cortisol. Foods rich in magnesium include dark-green leafy vegetables, cashews, almonds, and Epsom salt. Yes, an Epsom salt bath not only helps to relieve tense muscles, but it also helps increase your magnesium levels and reduces your stress. Another natural source of magnesium and a stress reliever is swimming in the ocean. Not only does the sight and sound of the ocean give you a feeling of calm and serenity, but swimming in it increases your magnesium levels. It helps relieve muscle tension and release stress. If you can't wait until that once-a-year vacation to somewhere tropical, find a saltwater pool in your area. Your body and mind will thank you.

Mindset

Louise Hay correlates shoulder problems with carrying the weight of the world on your shoulders and feeling like life is a burden.

Even if my intellect hasn't registered stress, my body lets me know. My first recognizable symptom is shoulder pain. It feels like a golf ball is in my right shoulder. No matter how much I may try to talk myself out of it or deny it, the body never lies. When I feel that, I know it is time to be more introspective on the cause. I think about what is going on in my life, and more importantly, how I honestly feel about it. I also use my Super Wonder Woman superpower of "no." I begin to say "no" to people's requests for favors and volunteering of my time. The key to this superpower is being okay with "no." Remember "no" is a complete sentence that can end with a period or exclamation point.

Affirmations

"Each day, I open my mind to the abundant opportunities that surround me."

"I am worthy of the very best in life. I now lovingly receive it."

"Every day and in every way, life is full of abundance."

"I choose to allow all my experiences to be joyous and loving."

STEP 7:
Release Resistance (Reproductive)

"When the womb is honored and respected, she becomes a channel of power, creativity, and beauty—it is the foundation of a woman's whole self."

—Queen Afua, *Sacred Woman: A Guide to Healing the Feminine Body, Mind and Spirit*

I had just made a major career change and was questioning my decision. Was this the right move? Will this make my life better? Did I make a mistake? I had so many questions and was questioning myself. As I was settling into a new reality, I discovered I had uterine fibroids. At first, they weren't giving me any problems, but then they began to grow and forever changed my life. Gradually, my menstrual cycles began to get longer and heavier. There were times I felt confined to the house for fear that I would have an embarrassing accident. I even started planning events and outings around my menstrual cycle. I didn't feel powerful or beautiful as referenced by Queen Afua. My womb had turned against me, and I felt like half a woman instead of a whole woman.

Many Super Wonder Women can relate to my experience. To get a better understanding of this journey and the influence of stress, you must understand the function of the reproductive system.

Function of the Reproductive System

The main function of the reproductive system is procreation and survival of humanity.

It does this by:

- producing mature eggs and sperm
- producing hormones (progesterone and estrogen in women, testosterone in men)
- nurturing the developing fetus

Female Reproductive System

The main structures of the female reproductive system are the vagina, uterus, fallopian tubes, ovaries, and breasts. The vagina serves as the receiver of the penis during intercourse, the birth canal, and the exit of products of menstruation. The uterus is a pear-shaped organ that consists of the cervix (what is being looked at and tested during a Pap smear) and the body. The fallopian tubes are tubes attached to the upper portion of the uterus and are approximately 10 cm in length. They serve as the meeting place for an egg that has been released from an ovary to connect with the lucky sperm. The ovaries are responsible for producing eggs and the hormones progesterone and estrogen.

Male Reproductive System

The organs of the male reproductive system include the penis, scrotum, testes, epididymis, prostate, and seminal vesicles. The scrotum houses the testes or testicles. This is where sperm and testosterone are produced. Once sperm is produced, it moves to the epididymis. The epididymis is composed of a network of tightly coiled tubes where the sperm matures and is stored. For the sperm to meet the egg to produce an offspring, it must be mixed with fluid called seminal fluid. Mature sperm moves to the seminal vesicles through a channel called the vas deferens. The seminal vesicles produce some of the fluid that contributes to semen.

Effect of Stress on Reproduction

Stress can be a doozy on your reproductive system and sex life; it decreases your libido, resulting in burnout in the bedroom. Sex is one of the healthiest (with the right person) and most pleasurable things you can do to release stress, but this can't happen if you have no desire.

Some of the repercussions of chronic stress extinguishing the fire in the bedroom:
- Alteration in hormones (testosterone, estrogen, and progesterone)
- Decreased lubrication
- Change in orgasm
- Decreased arousal

Stress also affects fertility, not just because there isn't any action, but also because it can disrupt ovulation (egg being released from the ovary in preparation to be fertilized) and is implicated in pre-term labor and miscarriages. A good friend of mine was trying for over a year to get pregnant without any success. The whole process was extremely stressful! Every month, she hoped and prayed for a miracle, only to see her dreaded "friend." She considered IVF (in vitro fertilization), which is a process in which eggs are taken from the mother and sperm from the father to combine in a laboratory. Once they have come together and the egg is successfully fertilized by the sperm to form the beginning of a fetus, it is transplanted back into the mother or a surrogate. Back to the story. My mother told her to relax and wait—she would not need fertility treatments. But you know anxiety and impatience. The couple made the appointment. A few days before the appointment, they found out she was pregnant au naturale. Once they relaxed some and let it flow, she conceived! Chronic stress doesn't just affect the female reproductive system. Fellas, it affects you too. You aren't going to want to hear this, but chronic stress can decrease testosterone levels, the amount of sperm produced, and even the size of your genitals! Release your stress and keep your package together!

Culinary Cure

Spices Spice It Up

Certain spices used commonly in the kitchen can spice up the bedroom. Hot and spicy cayenne is one of them, and so is parsley. Both are a good source of zinc, which is essential for testosterone production in men and women. Testosterone is what fuels the sex drive. Zinc also inhibits the secretion of our stress hormone cortisol.

Chocolate

Good news! I'm giving you a prescription to indulge a little bit. Yes, chocolate is good for the reproductive system because it increases libido. More specifically, a substance in chocolate called *theobromine* makes you feel stimulated and excited. The best chocolate in which to indulge is dark chocolate. The higher the cacao content, the better. Milk chocolate has more sugar, which if consumed in excessive amounts, can adversely affect the health of your reproductive system.

Mindset

According to Louise Hay, female problems are associated with denial of the self and rejecting the feminine aspects within. I view the female reproductive system as the microcosm of the universe. It is where creation happens and life is nurtured. Since all things are connected, problems in the reproductive system that are not due to chronic illness are reflective of creativity, femininity, resistance, and safety. Many women have experienced trauma, leaving them feeling powerless and unsafe. I recommend seeking a good therapist or counselor who can help you heal and reclaim your "power" from a time when you felt powerless. For others, reflect and meditate to find your voice, creativity, and passion. How do you feel about womanhood? Motherhood? Especially for those with uterine fibroids, what ideas, thoughts, and/or attitudes are you suppressing or resisting? In my case, every month when I saw evidence of "my friend" coming for a visit, my stress levels dramatically increased. Would this month be better or worse? What was I doing wrong to cause this to happen? How could I make it better? I had to take a long and hard look at myself and begin the process of honestly answering the questions: "How do I view myself as a woman? What patterns are repeatedly showing up in my life that I am resisting?" It was Carl Jung who first said, "What you resist persists." What aspects of yourself are you resisting instead of celebrating?

Affirmations

"I release the pattern in me that attracted this experience. I create only good in my life."

"I rejoice in the feminine. I love being a woman, and I love my body."

"I am fearfully and wonderfully made."

"I am a masterpiece."

STEP 8: Release Bitterness and Annoyance (Immune)

Many people are holding on to bitterness and unforgiveness. Oftentimes, the feeling is a one-way street. The other party or parties involved have moved on with their lives and have no idea you feel the way you do. Bitterness is like an open cut that never heals and continues to bleed and express pus. Our immune system is responsible for preventing or eradicating infection and helps us heal.

Function of the Immune System

The primary responsibility of the immune system is to protect against illnesses and diseases. It is our first line of defense against bacteria, viruses, fungi, parasites, and the big "C"—cancer. The immune system, also called the lymphatic system, is made up of the spleen, thymus, tonsils, adenoids, lymph nodes, bone marrow, and vessels. When the body recognizes something as "foreign," such as a virus that causes the flu or bacteria, it signals white blood cells (immune cells) to go to the area of infection. These cells are produced in the bone marrow and circulate in the blood, waiting for their assignment. There are many different types of white blood cells that have different functions. For example, two of my favorite types of white blood cells are macrophages and natural killer cells. Macrophages are distributed throughout the body on high alert, ready and waiting to spring into action. When a harmful organism such as a virus or bacterium is detected, it goes to the invader, surrounds it, and digests it to destroy it. This process is called phagocytosis (pha-go-si-toe-sis). Macrophages also recruit other types of immune cells to activate in the process. In addition, macrophages contribute to health maintenance by removing toxic material and debris from cells and tissues. For example, macrophages in the lungs remove allergic particles.

Natural killer (NK) cells are developed from cells in the bone marrow as well. They can be found circulating in the blood and liver and in the placenta of pregnant women. The power of these cells is their role in tumor and cancer prevention.

NK cells transport immune response cells such as white blood cells to the site in the body where they are needed to fight off infection and harmful mutated cells that cause diseases such as cancer. Think of them as assassins of malignant (bad) cells. When a cell has mutated or changed its structure to that of a harmful cell, if allowed to exponentially reproduce, it will develop into a tumor and cancer. The role of NK cells is to prevent this from happening. When a malignant cell or cell that has been infected by a virus or bacterium is detected in the body, the NK cells activate. They release a specific type of protein that induces instant cell death, or what is known as apoptosis (a-pop-toe-sis). The wonder of this process is that NK cells only target malignant or infected cells while sparing healthy cells.

Effect of Stress on the Immune System

Studies show that short-term stress lasting for minutes or hours is beneficial to our immune system and can actually give it a boost. Short-term stress causes immune cells to mobilize to the areas where they are needed most, such as the skin. This is referred to as "immune readiness."

However, chronic stress lasting for weeks or months is detrimental. Chronic stress can decrease the number of immune cells circulating in the body as well as their activity. For example, the activity of NK cells decreases, making you more susceptible to tumor formation, growth of existing tumors, and/or cancer. It can also:

- increase the time for wounds to heal
- reactivate dormant herpes virus
- increase risk of infections, such as colds

I knew someone who was experiencing many life changes, creating a tremendous amount of stress. They were going through a separation from their spouse and more duties at work, covering the responsibilities for two positions. My friend had a sinus infection for over a year! After numerous rounds of antibiotics, Flonase, Claritin, and even steroids, the infection waxed and waned but was never completely eradicated. Finally, they committed time to their self-care and scheduled a two-week destination vacation. Upon return,

I instantly witnessed a complete change in their demeanor, a glow in their skin, and guess what else? No sinus issues!

Culinary Cure

Vitamin C

Vitamin C enhances the health of our immune system by increasing the production of white blood cells. As previously discussed, Vitamin C can help regulate cortisol spikes when the stress response is activated. Citrus fruits are the first thing that come to mind when thinking of Vitamin C rich foods. However, dark-green leafy vegetables are rich sources of Vitamin C as well. Our parents were on to something when they said, "You need to eat your green vegetables every day." You get more bang for your buck!

Zinc

Zinc is necessary for adequate functioning of the immune system. Sufficient levels are needed for the full functioning of white blood cells such as macrophages and NK cells. Therefore, a zinc deficiency makes you more prone to infections and other illnesses. Zinc also inhibits the secretion of cortisol, helping to mitigate the multitude of adverse effects from high levels of cortisol due to chronic stress. One of my favorite soothing sources of zinc is chamomile tea. For those a little more adventurous, oysters are also a good source of zinc.

Mindset

According to Louise Hay, issues with the immune system, such as infection, are associated with feelings of irritation or annoyance about a recent situation. Sinus problems in particular are symbolic of irritation with someone, commonly someone close to you.

Like the above example, amazing things happen when you commit to your self-care and peace of mind. Sometimes you have to jump outside of your comfort zone to attain your peace and calm and then defend it. You deserve it! Committing to your peace and calm helps you release irritation and annoyance with situations and people. It shifts your mindset to allow you to accept that you can't control others' behavior, so no need to allow it to change you

Affirmations

"I choose to be peaceful and harmonious."

"I choose to declare peace and harmony with all the individuals around me. I surround myself with love and goodwill."

"I choose to create sweetness in my life."

STEP 9:
Release Control (Endocrine)

Control Freak: a person whose behavior indicates a powerful need to control people or circumstances in everyday matters (*Merriam-Webster*).

> *Me: "Hi, my name is Dr. Michelle."*
> *Recovery Group: "Hi, Dr. Michelle."*
> *Me: "And I'm a recovering perfectionist."*

Liking everything "perfect" and not trusting anyone else to do something is a telltale sign of a control freak. Being a control freak is exhausting and extremely stressful because you never allow yourself a break. You believe that the only way to ensure something is done correctly is to do it yourself.

Now what does the endocrine system have to do with control, you ask? The endocrine system is part of an integrative approach of psychiatry, psychology, endocrinology, and neuroscience (study of the nervous system) called psychoneuroendocrinology (sy-co-new-ro-en-doe-crin-ol-ogy). Basically, it is the study of how hormonal changes influence behavior, psychological well-being, and the health of the nervous system. For example, post-partum depression comes under the heading of a psychoneuroendocrinological issue; the massive fluctuation in hormone levels leads to depression, adversely affecting psychological well-being.

Function of the Endocrine System

The endocrine system is made up of different glands in your body that produce and secrete hormones. It includes the hypothalamus, pituitary gland, pineal gland, thyroid, parathyroid, ovaries, testes, pancreas, and adrenal glands. These endocrine glands have an amazing communication network that acts like a looped factory line. The endocrine system is responsible for producing or regulating hormones that regulate blood sugars, body temperature, reproduction, and metabolism, just to name a few. The activity in one endocrine gland, in most cases, affects the other ones. Two we will discuss here are the thyroid gland and the pancreas.

The three hormones the thyroid produces are T2 (diiodothyronine), T3 (triiodothyronine), and T4 (thyroxine). These hormones secreted by the thyroid interact with other hormones, including insulin, cortisol, estrogen, progesterone, and testosterone. The active thyroid hormone, T3, influences metabolism, cholesterol levels, body temperature, appetite, digestion, menstruation, fertility, and energy levels. Thyroid hormone levels also affect the adrenal glands. Adrenal glands are small glands that sit on top of the kidneys. They produce hormones such as cortisol and adrenaline.

The pancreas is an organ with two main functions: digestion and blood sugar regulation. The pancreas produces enzymes that help break down fat, protein, and carbohydrates.

Effect of Stress on the Endocrine System

When we are stressed, the hypothalamus sends a signal to the pituitary gland, which in turn sends a signal to the thyroid gland and adrenal glands. This sets off a cascade of events affecting the production or levels of the hormones these glands control. With chronic stress, levels of cortisol and adrenaline from the adrenal glands are increased, which somewhat decreases thyroid function, simulating underactive thyroid or hypothyroid. When the thyroid is out of whack, it can wreak havoc on digestion, menstruation, metabolism, body temperature, blood pressure, and blood sugar. How, you ask? Your thyroid function is intimately tied to your adrenal function, which is intimately affected by how you handle stress. You *need more thyroid hormones during stressful times.*

Culinary Cure

Fruits High in Antioxidants

The saying goes, "the darker the berry, the sweeter the juice." The darker-colored berries, such as blueberries and raspberries, as well as other fruits we love, such as cherries and red grapes, are great sources of antioxidants, especially the antioxidant Vitamin C. Recall that Vitamin C is our go-to preventive prescription for stress. In addition, red grapes and blueberries are rich sources of another antioxidant called resveratrol, which is beneficial for the health of the pancreas.

Iodine

Iodine is necessary for thyroid hormone production. In addition, iodine may be depleted with chronic stress. Two foods rich in iodine are sea vegetables, such as nori or dulse and fish. Cod and haddock have higher amounts of iodine. Have Sushi Night Saturday to relax and rejuvenate your thyroid.

Mindset

Because the endocrine system's glands produce hormones that influence just about every organ system, it, along with the brain, can be thought of as a control center. The endocrine system can remind us to release control of the things we can't change and focus on changing our minds to change our life. On my journey of self-discovery to live a stress FREELIFE, I learned that the more I held on tightly to something to control it, my hand was clenched too tightly to receive anything else.

> *Got my own mind*
> *I want to make my own decisions*
> *When it has to do with my life, my life*
> *I wanna be the one in control*
>
> – "Control" by Janet Jackson

I remember back in the day, the older people used to say, "You need to get some business." Translation: you wouldn't have time to worry about what others are doing and try to control their lives if you put the needed attention on your own life and on building yourself up. Focus only on controlling your mind, your thoughts, your actions, and your life. This is fundamental to living a stress FREELIFE!

Affirmations

"I alone am in control of myself and everything I alone choose to think, feel, say, and do."

"I am in control of my life by the choices I make."

"I control my thoughts. My thoughts do not control me."

"I am calm and relaxed. I allow others to be who they are, how they are.

STEP 10: Release Anxiety (Skin)

According to Louise Hay, skin conditions are associated with anxiety, fear, feeling threatened, and the lack of self-acceptance. Think about it—when a pimple breaks out on your face, no matter how small it is, you believe that it looks like the Grand Canyon on your face. You feel anxious and self-conscious that everyone is staring at it and it has distracted them from really hearing and seeing you. More than a reflection of beauty and identity, skin has very important functions.

Function of the Skin System

The skin is considered the largest organ on our bodies. It functions mainly as protection from harmful bacteria, toxic substances, and UV radiation. Another important function includes helping regulate body temperature through sweating and sensation (heat, cold, pressure, pain).

Effect of Stress on the Skin System

The mind and the skin are connected. Scientists have coined the phrase *psycho-dermatologic* disorders, an interaction between the mind and the skin, which can precipitate a skin condition or make an existing one worse due to emotional stress. Maybe you have experienced it before a big presentation; overnight, a huge pimple appeared on your face like you were going through puberty! You scream, "I can't believe this! Why is this happening?!" Why? Because when cortisol levels are high, there is an increase in oil production in the glands of your skin (sebaceous glands).

Stress can also cause a flare-up of skin conditions like psoriasis and eczema. I've seen this happen in my younger cousins with eczema. Before college midterms or finals, their eczema will flare up.

Emotional stress can also cause hair breakage or loss. For years before I started this work with stress release, I had a stress point right at the top of my head.

The hair would grow only to a certain length and then would just thin out. It wasn't until I stopped perming my hair and finding creative and natural ways to release my stress that my hair started growing in thick, even in that location.

For those of us who are vain, please release what is keeping you up at night; look in the mirror—it is aging you. Seriously, high cortisol levels that occur with chronic stress lead to a decrease in skin elasticity, which is what keeps it looking youthful and resilient.

Culinary Cure

People often ask me, "What do you use on your skin? It looks so smooth and clear and is glowing." I always reply, "It's not what I put on it, it's what I put in."

Avocados

I absolutely LOVE avocados, which are rich in Vitamin E, which helps the skin repair itself. Avocados are one of my secret weapons to maintain my youthful glow. Just as the saying goes, "The eyes are the windows to the soul," the skin is a reflection of your wellness. Avocados also contain "good fat," which help moisturize the skin and keep it soft and supple. Avocados are a great source of B vitamins, which are necessary to calm and maintain a healthy nervous system, thus relieving stress. When something or someone is on your "last nerve," have an avocado. Avocados are a rich source of the amino acids tyrosine and tryptophan, which are necessary to produce neurotransmitters (brain chemicals), such as dopamine and serotonin, respectively. These neurotransmitters regulate mood and those "feel good" sensations. Next time you go to happy hour to unwind, make sure you get the guacamole and chips.

Sweet Potatoes

Sweet potatoes are considered a skin superfood. Their high content of Vitamin A and beta-carotene are what help defy skin aging by combating free radical damage. Plus, sweet potatoes are rich in Vitamin C, which helps relieve stress by preventing cortisol spikes that occur with the stress response.

Mindset

Per the psychology dictionary, anxiety is:

a mood state characterized by worry, apprehension, and somatic symptoms, similar to the tension caused when an individual anticipates impending danger, catastrophe, or misfortune. The threat the person is responding to may be real or imagined or internal or external. It may be an identifiable situation or a more vague fear of the unknown.

Often, people are anxious not of actual occurrences, but of possible occurrences and outcomes. How many times before attempting something new have you been filled with anxiety and fear? You play a scenario of failure and falling over and over in your head. MINDSET! You can shift your mindset from one of impending doom to certainty of success. I once read a pneumonic: F-E-A-R: Face Everything And Rise! Visualize yourself winning, succeeding, and rising!

Affirmations

"I lovingly protect myself with thoughts of joy and peace."

"With every breath, I release the anxiety within me, and I become more and more calm."

"I overcome my fear of anything and everything and live life courageously."

"I am free of anxiety and continue to be so."

STEP 11:
Release Unforgiveness and Bitterness (Heart)

"Our hearts are all prison walls when we hold people captive with chains of unforgiveness."

–Ikechukwu Izuakor

Often people who hold on to unforgiveness develop bitterness towards the person or situation, which eventually can lead to what is referred to as a "hardened heart." The sweetness found in love and relationships is missing. It's as if they are imprisoned by their bitterness and the freedom of life is blocked. According to Carsten Wrosch of Concordia University in Montreal, bitter, angry people have higher blood pressure and heart rate and are more likely to die of heart disease and other illnesses.

Function of the Cardiovascular System

The primary function of the cardiovascular system is the flow and transport of blood, oxygen, nutrients, and other substances throughout the body. Its main components are the heart, blood vessels (arteries and veins), and blood. Amazingly, the heart beats approximately 100,000 times per day and pumps approximately five quarts of blood throughout your body.

Effect of Stress on the Cardiovascular System

One of the most detrimental effects of stress on your cardiovascular health is high blood pressure. Chronic stress increases both the systolic (top number) and diastolic (bottom number) pressure. The main culprit is what is called vasoconstriction (smaller openings of the blood vessels) caused by sustained high cortisol levels. Think of a water hose on at full force. When you tighten it, what happens? The water flows out slower and increases pressure in the hose. Same concept. When you startle someone or give them disturbing news and they say, "Oh Lord, you got my pressure up!" they are telling the truth.

In cases of extreme and sudden stress, such as the death of a loved one, car accident or other accident,

natural disaster, intense fear, or unexpected bad news, "broken heart syndrome" can occur. The Japanese call it takotsubo. It presents like a heart attack with chest pain, shortness of breath, and even damage to the heart muscle that looks like heart failure. "Broken heart syndrome" typically occurs in women, but unlike a true heart attack, symptoms and damage usually reverse within one month.

Culinary Cure

Beans

The darker-colored beans, such as black, kidney, or red beans, are a rich source of B vitamins and zinc, which are not only good for heart health, but also the health and strength of the nervous system to facilitate managing stress. Beans and legumes are also a rich source of fiber and protein, which is good news for my stressed-out vegetarian friends. For these reasons, beans contribute to cardiovascular health, reducing the risk of heart disease and high cholesterol.

Fish

The omega-3 fatty acids in fish help lower blood pressure and cholesterol. Consistent intake of omega-3 fatty acids is also shown to decrease the risk of heart attack, stroke, abnormal heart rhythms, and atherosclerosis (hardening of the arteries). Due to these health benefits, the American Heart Association suggests eating fish twice a week. The best kind is wild-caught marine fish, such as salmon, halibut, or cod.

Mindset

"A prolonged unforgiveness is a prolonged destruction mindset."

–Sunday Adelaja

The heart is the place of your innermost feelings and character. When it is full of unforgiveness and bitterness, it robs you of the joy and sweetness of life. My paternal grandmother, as accomplished, intelligent, and God-fearing as she was, held grudges for years. My entire life, I never felt that I really connected with her as I expected a grandmother and her only granddaughter should. She also had a heart condition. My daddy and one of my favorite aunts (my grandmother's oldest sister) were with my grandmother as she took her last breaths. My aunt told me that the entire time she sat there trying to support and comfort my grandmother, she never acknowledged her. She would acknowledge her other visitors as they came and went, but never my aunt. My grandmother and aunt had friction for most of their lives. My aunt told me she did not even know why. As my grandmother took her last breaths, mostly gasps, she transitioned with unforgiveness in her heart, never taking a moment to show love, forgiveness, peace, or compassion towards my aunt. Her transition into eternity was not smooth or pleasant. My daddy said he would not wish that on anybody.

What is blocking you from the abundance of joy in your life? What conversations do you need to have and need support and an extra push to do so? Whom can you release in love and wish them their highest good as you ascend to yours?

"An open heart has greater power than a clenched fist."
–Matshona Dhliwayo

Affirmations

"I forgive everyone in my past for all perceived wrongs. I release them with LOVE."

"I am grateful for the basics in life: forgiveness, courage, LOVE, and laughter."

"I forgive myself, and it becomes easier to forgive."

"I am forgiving, loving, gentle, and kind, and I know that life loves me."

STEP 12:
The Super Wonder Woman's Stress FREELIFE Strategy

Congratulations on taking a step forward in releasing stress and reclaiming YOU! Not the "you" that everyone sees, but the "you" that you have always known yourself to be but was buried under mountains of worry, anxiety, doubt, and fear.

Stress and the stress response influence every system in the body and have the ability to affect every area of our lives. Short-term stress, at times, can be beneficial. When completing a presentation or a report or before a speaking engagement, short-term stress would be beneficial. This gives us an understanding of why people say, "I work best under pressure." It can be the spark and the force that drives us to achieve more, improve the quality of our life, ask for a raise, or complete 36 hours of work in 20. I know it has been challenging to get up every day, put on your lipstick, your cape, and your game face, and go out there and "conquer the world."

But if we conquer the chaos and direct the stress, it can push us to grow, to change, to fight, to dream big, to achieve those dreams, and to adapt to an ever-changing internal and external environment without breaking a sweat or soiling our cape. This is the life of a Super Wonder Woman.

By exploring and implementing these twelve steps to release dis-harmony and disease, you can create your stress FREELIFE strategy! Be encouraged. You are not alone and do not have to do it alone. There are other Super Wonder Women who will hold your cape if you need to cry or hold your hand when you need to repeat a step. And as your sister Super Wonder Woman, I'm here to help you conquer your chaos by transforming your tension to tranquility and burnout to balance.

Now go forth and be brilliant!

"When we are no longer able to change a situation, we are challenged to change ourselves."

—Viktor E. Frankl

Thank You

I am the answer to my great-great-great-grandmother's prayers. I would like to thank all of the Super Wonder Women in my life who prepared the way and made me the woman I am today. And to the Super Men standing next to them who have protected and offered strong arms to envelope when hurting. I'd like to give a special thank you to my mother, Ellaine Sue Jackson Clay, who always told me to walk like I knew where I was going, even if I didn't, with my head held high. And to the most phenomenal Super Wonder Woman I have ever seen grace this planet, my grandmother Martha Louise Black Jackson, affectionately known as "Nanny." She taught me how to carry myself like a lady at all times, especially in the face of trying and tense times. She showed me not only how to don a cape like a true Super Wonder Woman, but how to make one with the creativity of my hands. I've watched the elder women in my life leap over challenging circumstances in a single bound with a smile and a prayer of faith. With their strength, prayers, faith, examples, and words of encouragement, I can too. And you can too.

Together, we can ignite your Super Wonder Woman superpowers to create your "burnout to balance" blueprint to your stress FREELIFE. Visit www.freelifestrategy.com.

Let's stay connected so we can fly free together!

Website: www.freelife7le.com
Facebook: www.wellnesswowfactor.com
Twitter: @drmichelleclay
Instagram: @drmichelleclay

About the Author

Dr. Michelle Clay's life mission is to empower professionals and overachievers to transform their lives from stressful, unbalanced, and unhealthy to happy, harmonious, and purposeful. She earned her bachelor of science in biology from Xavier University of Louisiana and her doctor of osteopathic medicine from Ohio University. She is also a certified holistic health counselor and clinical nutritionist and the coauthor of *The Making of a Medical Mogul: Volume 1*. Dr. Michelle loves volunteering (she has volunteered with Dress for Success New Orleans, Habitat for Humanity, and Food for the Poor), traveling, reading, crocheting, cooking, and the ocean. She lives in New Orleans, Louisiana, with her fiancé and their cat, Boumba.

To connect, visit her website at
www.freelife7le.com

CREATING DISTINCTIVE BOOKS
WITH INTENTIONAL RESULTS

We're a collaborative group of creative masterminds with a mission to produce high-quality books to position you for monumental success in the marketplace.

Our professional team of writers, editors, designers, and marketing strategists work closely together to ensure that every detail of your book is a clear representation of the message in your writing.

Want to know more?
Write to us at info@publishyourgift.com
or call (888) 949-6228

Discover great books, exclusive offers, and more at
www.PublishYourGift.com

Connect with us on social media

@publishyourgift

www.ingramcontent.com/pod-product-compliance
Lightning Source LLC
Chambersburg PA
CBHW041958080526
44588CB00021B/2792